5-12
2002

To

My Baby Sister, Dora

With Love

From Big Sister

On

Jesusa

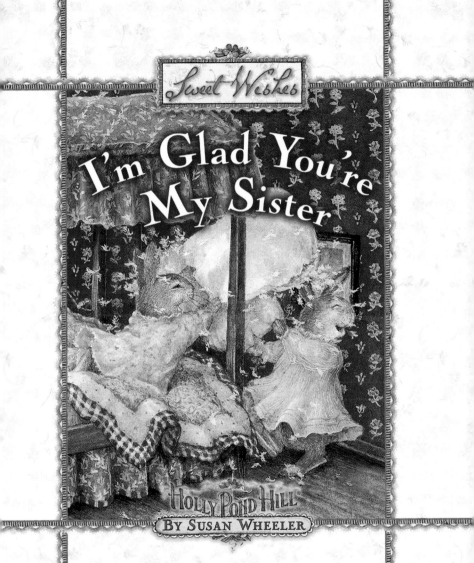

Sweet Wishes

I'm Glad You're My Sister

HOLLY POND HILL

By Susan Wheeler

HARVEST HOUSE PUBLISHERS
Eugene, Oregon

I'm Glad You're My Sister

Text Copyright © 2002 by Harvest House Publishers
Eugene, Oregon 97402

ISBN 0-7369-0787-4

Design and production by Garborg Design Works, Minneapolis, Minnesota

Scripture quotations are taken from the Holy Bible, New International Version®, Copyright © 1973, 1978, 1984 by the International Bible Society. Used by permission of Zondervan Publishing House.

Printed in Hong Kong

02 03 04 05 06 07 08 09 10 / NG / 10 9 8 7 6 5 4 3 2 1

A sister is a gift to the heart,

A friend to the spirit,

A golden thread to the meaning of life.

ISADORA JAMES

For there is no friend like a sister;

In calm or stormy weather;

To cheer one on the tedious way,

To fetch one if one goes astray,

To lift one if one totters down,

To strengthen whilst one stands.

CHRISTINA ROSSETTI

A ministering angel shall my sister be.

WILLIAM SHAKESPEARE

Both within the family and without, our sisters hold up our mirrors: our images of who we are and of who we can dare to become.

ELIZABETH FISHEL

Then come, my Sister!
come, I pray,
With speed put on
your woodland dress;
And bring no book:
for this one day
We'll give to idleness.

WILLIAM WORDSWORTH
To My Sister

With a sister by your side, you can always count on someone who knew you as you were and loves you as you are.

AUTHOR UNKNOWN

Susan Wheeler

Sisters is probably the most competitive relationship within the family, but once sisters are grown, it becomes the strongest relationship.

MARGARET MEAD

Sisters are for sharing
laughter and wiping tears.

AUTHOR UNKNOWN

Is solace anywhere more comforting

than in the arms of a sister?

ALICE WALKER

Sisters touch your heart
in ways no other could. Sisters
share...their hopes, their fears,
their love, everything they have.
Real friendship springs from
their special bonds.

CARRIE BAGWELL

Chance made us sisters, hearts made us friends.

AUTHOR UNKNOWN

The family is one of nature's masterpieces.

GEORGE SANTAYANA

*Charm is deceptive,
and beauty is fleeting;
but a woman who fears the
LORD is to be praised.*

THE BOOK OF PROVERBS

She is a bowl of
golden water
which brims but
never overflows.

ISADORA JAMES

Sisters are special
From young ones to old.
God gave me a sister
More precious than gold.

AUTHOR UNKNOWN

There was once a child, and he strolled about a good deal, and thought of a number of things. He had a sister, who was a child, too, and his constant companion. These two used to wonder all day long. They wondered at the beauty of the flowers; they wondered at the height and blueness of the sky; they wondered at the depth of the bright water; they wondered at the goodness and the power of God who made the lovely world.

CHARLES DICKENS
A CHILD'S DREAM OF A STAR

*Sisters make the real conversations...
not the saying but the never needing
to say is what counts.*

MARGARET LEE RUNBECK

$\mathcal{A}$ sister's a friend who brings laughter your way,

She supports you in all that you do,

She's been at the heart of so many glad moments

And shares precious memories with you...

She knows how you've changed,

How you've grown through the years,

And she knows all that you're dreaming of.

She's the comfort of family, the warm touch of

home...She's the beautiful blessing of love.

AUTHOR UNKNOWN

Many women

do noble things,

but you surpass

them all.

THE BOOK OF PROVERBS

Sisters...

soulmates for life.

VERONICA CURTIS

I cannot deny that now that I am without your company, I feel not only that I am deprived of a very dear sister, but that I have lost half of myself.

BEATRICE D'ESTE

The desire to be and have a sister is a primitive and profound one that may have everything or nothing to do with the family a woman is born to. It is a desire to know and be known by someone who shares blood and body, history and dreams...

ELIZABETH FISHEL

The day God blessed us with you,

Was truly a gift to us all.

He gave me someone

Who He knew would

Always love me,

Someone I could talk to,

Share my life with,

Laugh with at all times,

Especially when I needed it most.

What God gave me was you!

My sister...my best friend.

DANA LYNN

26

"I don't see how you can write and act such splendid things, Jo. You're a regular Shakespeare!" exclaimed Beth, who firmly believed that her sisters were gifted with wonderful genius in all things. In spite of her small vanities, Margaret had a sweet and pious nature, which unconsciously influenced her sisters, especially Jo, who loved her very tenderly, and obeyed her because her advice was so gently given. The two older girls were a great deal to one another, but each took one of the younger sisters into her keeping and watched over her in her own way, "playing mother" they called it, and put their sisters in the places of discarded dolls with the maternal instinct of little women.

LOUISA MAY ALCOTT
LITTLE WOMEN

We shared many secrets,
the same mom and dad,
We shared lots of good times,
don't think of the bad.
Our memories we'll cherish,
with love without end,
I'm glad you're my
sister, I'm glad you're
my friend.

AUTHOR UNKNOWN

28

The sister bond is
often greater than that
with a friend or brother.

DR. HARRIETTE MCADOO

And when I started to cry, she sluiced back my hair with her fingers. "We're always sisters," she said quietly, and then I shut my eyes, and then I didn't hear the phone ring anymore. Instead I gripped the hand she offered me, holding fast to her...

CAROLINE LEAVITT
THE WRONG SISTER

"*My dear Jane!*" exclaimed Elizabeth, "*you are too good. Your sweetness and disinterestedness are really angelic; I do not know what to say to you. I feel as if I have never done you justice, or loved you as you deserve.*"

JANE AUSTEN
PRIDE AND PREJUDICE

She is very fair, my little sister.

ELIZABETH ROBINS

So they sent their sister Rebekah on her way…And they blessed Rebekah and said to her, "Our sister, may you increase to thousands upon thousands…"

THE BOOK OF GENESIS

Ever since Laura could remember, Carrie had been her little sister. First she had been a tiny baby, then she had been Baby Carrie, then she had been a clutcher and tagger, always asking "Why?" Now she was ten years old, old enough to be really a sister.

LAURA INGALLS WILDER
THE LONG WINTER

3 4

Will laughed at, accepted graciously, and didn't obey; but he liked it, and trudged away for another week's work, rested, cheered, and strengthened by that quiet, happy day with Polly, for he had been brought up to believe in home influences, and this brother and sister loved one another dearly, and were not ashamed to own it.

LOUISA MAY ALCOTT
AN OLD-FASHIONED GIRL

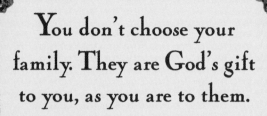

You don't choose your family. They are God's gift to you, as you are to them.

DESMOND TUTU

My sister shares a part of me...

that no one else shall ever see.

And when the days and miles divide us...

the bond we have will live inside us.

Together sharing dreams, love, and laughter...

My sister for always, my friend...forever.

AUTHOR UNKNOWN

A sister can be seen as someone
who is both ourselves and very
much not ourselves—a special double.

TONI MORRISON

I sought my soul, but my soul I could not see.

I sought my God, but my God eluded me.

I sought my sisters, and I found all three.

AUTHOR UNKNOWN

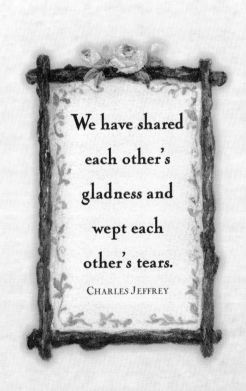

We have shared
each other's
gladness and
wept each
other's tears.

CHARLES JEFFREY

So much of what is best

in us is bound up

in our love of family, that

it remains the

measure of our stability

because it measures

our sense of loyalty. All

other pacts of love or fear

derive from it and are

modeled upon it.

DANIEL LONG

Having a sister is like having a best friend you can't get rid of. You know whatever you do, they'll still be there.

AMY LI

For many years we've shared our lives
One roof we once lived under.
Sometimes we laughed, sometimes we cried,
Through winter storms and thunder.
The younger years have faded fast,
We've gone our separate ways.
But through all time our friendship lasts
Our bond in life remains.
As summer brings the happy times,
The autumn winds will whisper:
A closer friend I'd never find
Than the one I call my sister.

AUTHOR UNKNOWN

What greater thing is there for human souls than to feel that they are joined for life—to be with each other in silent, unspeakable memories.

GEORGE ELIOT

44

What one loves in childhood
stays in the heart forever.

MARY JO PUTNEY

*There is a space within
sisterhood for likeness and
difference, for the subtle differences
that challenge and delight...*

CHRISTINE DOWNING

45

Susan
Whee[...]

*P*lease, God, let me have a baby sister...I repeated it over and over like that, the way I heard people at church do, under my breath, kind of like a whisper. It seemed like forever before the phone rang, but when it did, we all jumped. Aunt Sophie knocked the handset off the wall as she ran to get it. She seemed scared.

"Hello?" Her voice was shaky. "Yes...*really!* Oh, thank God! How long? Uh-huh. How big?"

My insides were spinning. *Please, God, let me have a baby sister. . .Please, God, let me have a baby sister...*

Aunt Sophie hung up the receiver and spun around just in time to see Joey sticking his tongue out at the phone. I was glad for it, too, because he was finally going to get it! But Aunt Sophie didn't seem to notice.

"Kids, go get washed up. We're going down to the hospital to see your new baby sister!"

My new baby sister? It worked!

MARGARET BECKER
GROWING UP TOGETHER

Sisters by chance.

Friends by choice.

AUTHOR UNKNOWN